Montessori abc's

Words by Christina Clemer
Photography by Nick Karwoski

Montessori abc's – How are they different?

The way Montessori teaches the alphabet is fundamentally different than other preschool methods. Montessori first teaches the phonetic sounds of each letter, rather than the names of each letter.

Learning the phonetic sounds really sets children up for success when it's time to learn to read. They have a firm grasp on the sound each letter makes and thus find it easier to string those sounds together to form words.

This focus on phonetic sounds makes it difficult to find a Montessori friendly alphabet book though! Most abc books use words that are not a phonetic representation of the letter (for instance, "giraffe" for "g" or "celery" for "c"). This is confusing for a child learning the phonetic sounds!

This led us to create this Montessori alphabet book for parents who are interested in teaching the alphabet and reading the Montessori way. In this book, each letter is shown with an image and word starting with the *phonetic* sound of the letter.

Another difference between Montessori and other methods is Montessori's focus on simplicity and reality-based learning. While many alphabet books have lots of images crammed on to one page, this one presents one photographic image per sound. This simplicity allows the child to really focus on the sound for each letter.

Why are the letters red and blue?

In Montessori, vowels and consonants are presented in contrasting colors.

This contrast helps children notice the difference between vowels and consonants and identify the common patterns in our language (for example, consonant-vowel-consonant is the pattern of many of the early phonetic words children learn).

Want to know more?

Please see the end of the book for ideas on how to use this book and how to encourage an interest in letters and please refer to my website, montessoriishmom.com for more resources, such as a guide to the phonetic alphabet and sample language activities you can do with your child.

apple

baby

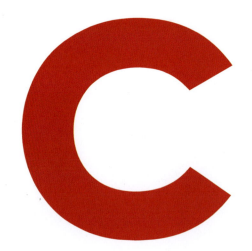

COW

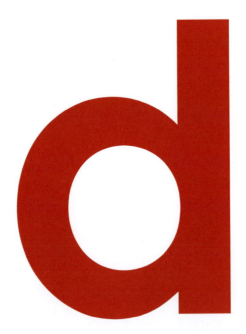

duck

elephant

frog

goat

h

hands

insect

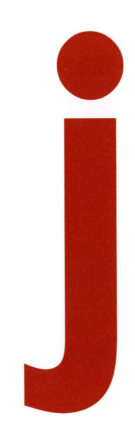

jackal

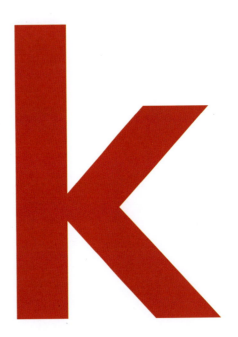

koala

monkey

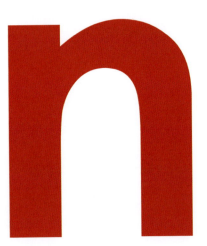

n

nail

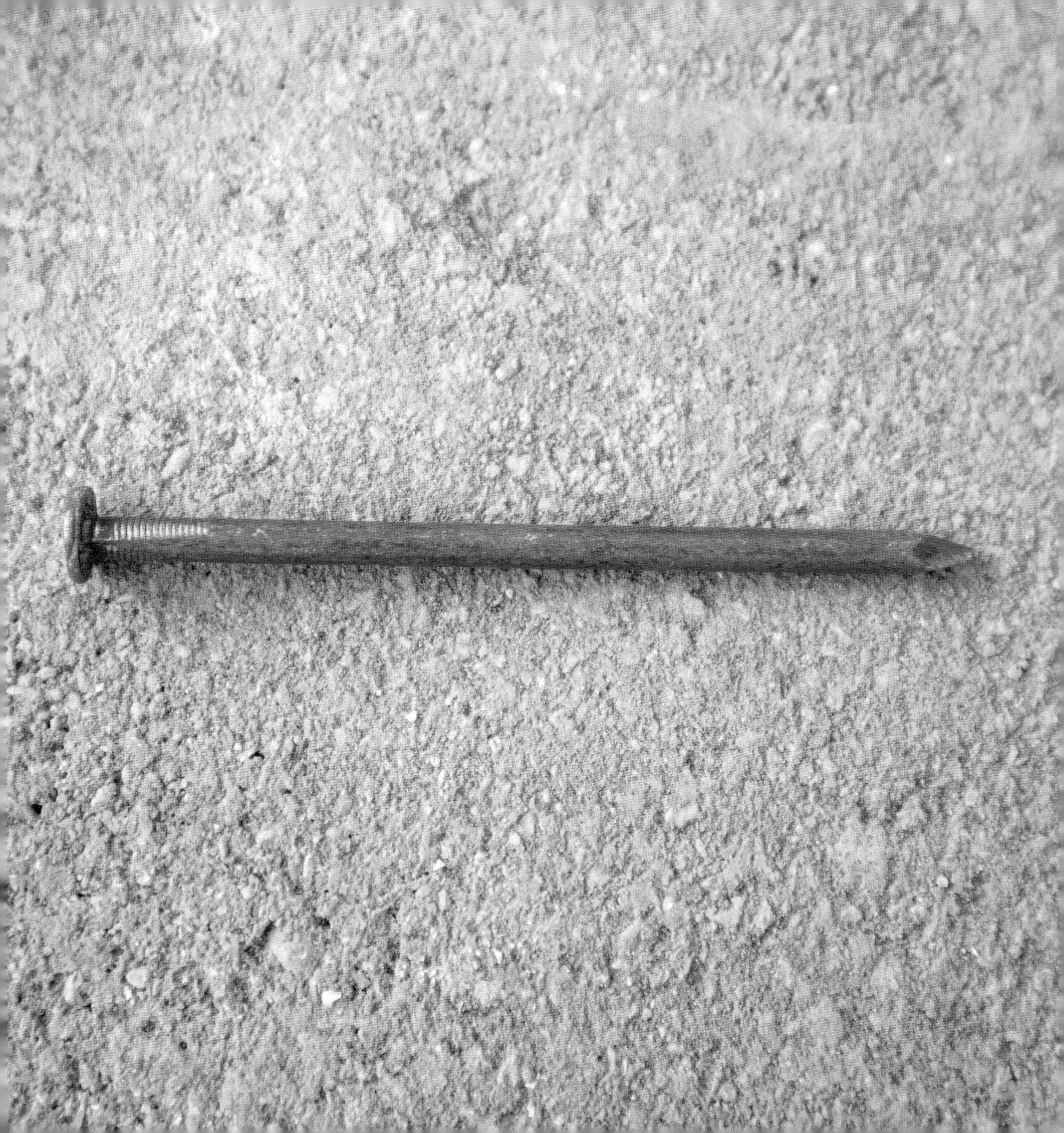

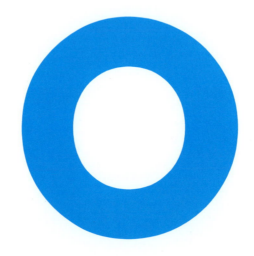

ostrich

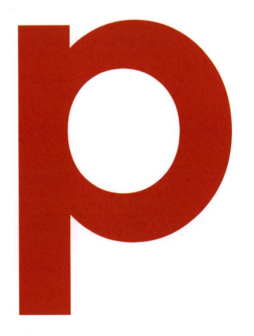

pumpkin

quilt

rhino

snake

train

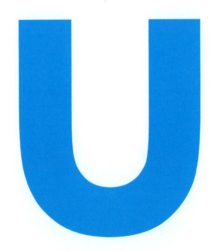

umbrella

vine

warthog

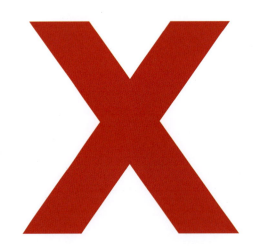

x-ray

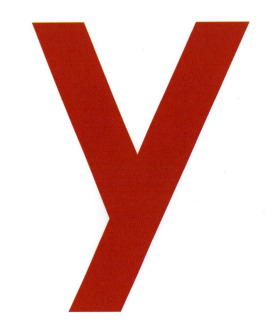

yucca

Z

zebra

"Our aim is not merely to make the child understand, and still less to force him to memorize, but so to touch his imagination as to enthuse him to his innermost core."

- Maria Montessori

If you're familiar with Montessori, you know that the approach does not use techniques such as flash cards or memorization. Rather Montessori focuses on providing children with the resources necessary to lead their own learning. As parents or teachers, we provide beautiful materials to inspire curiosity and the children take the lead.

Thus, this book is not meant to be used "flashcard-style," quizzing children on each letter. Instead, observe your child and notice when they show an interest in letters. They may start pointing to the tiny writing on the bottom of a favorite toy or asking what a letter on a puzzle says. This is the perfect time to start sharing letter activities and books with your child.

This book can of course be used before that interest emerges as well, just casually say the sound for each letter and discuss the images with your child.

When they do truly start to show an interest in letters, you can use each page as a jumping off point. Make the "a" sound and say something like, "Apple starts with 'a,' let's think of some other things that start with the 'a' sound".

Your child will likely let you take the lead at first, but if you keep playing games like this, they will join in with enthusiasm!

About the Author:

Christina Clemer is an American Montessori Society (AMS) certified teacher for 3-6 year olds. She attended Montessori school for 10 years herself before going on to graduate from Georgetown University. She has experience teaching in Montessori classrooms as well as writing about Montessori for sites including Mother.ly and TheTot.com. She also writes a blog, montessoriishmom.com, where she chronicles her Montessori exploits at home with her two young children, James and Lilah.

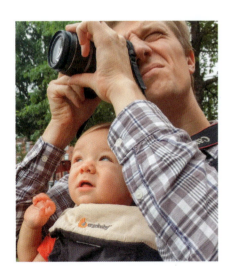

About the Photographer:

Nick Karwoski is a father and cycle touring enthusiast who pursues nature photography in his spare time.

See more of his work at nickkarwoski.com.

Printed in Great Britain
by Amazon